BUDDY

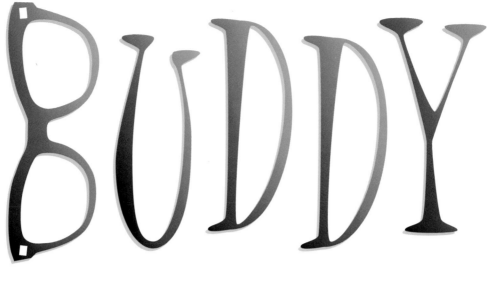

The Story of Buddy Holly

written by
Anne Bustard ♩♩ Kurt Cyrus
illustrated by

A Paula Wiseman Book

SIMON & SCHUSTER BOOKS FOR YOUNG READERS

New York   London   Toronto   Sydney

To my parents, who encouraged me to dream big—A. B.

The author gratefully acknowledges the assistance of the Buddy Holly Center; Lauren Flick, a patient older sister; Bill Griggs; her writing buddies, Kathi Appelt, Dianna Aston, Betty X. Davis, Meredith Davis, Jimmy Hendricks, Debbie Leland, Cynthia Leitich Smith, Greg Leitich Smith, and Jerry Wermund; her agent, Rosemary Stimola; and her editor, Paula Wiseman.

SIMON & SCHUSTER BOOKS FOR YOUNG READERS
An imprint of Simon & Schuster Children's Publishing Division
1230 Avenue of the Americas, New York, New York 10020
Text copyright © 2005 by Anne Bustard
Illustrations copyright © 2005 by Kurt Cyrus
SIMON & SCHUSTER BOOKS FOR YOUNG READERS is a trademark of Simon & Schuster, Inc.
Book design by Greg Stadnyk
The text for this book is set in Pike.
The illustrations for this book are rendered in watercolors, ink, and colored pencils.
Manufactured in China
10 9 8 7 6 5 4 3 2 1
Library of Congress Cataloging-in-Publication Data
Bustard, Anne, 1951–
Buddy : the Buddy Holly story / Anne Bustard ; illustrated by Kurt Cyrus.
p. cm.
"A Paula Wiseman Book."
Summary: A biography of the musician, born Charles Hardin Holley during the Depression in Texas, who pioneered a new kind of music.
ISBN 0-689-86667-4
1. Holly, Buddy, 1936-1959–Juvenile literature. 2. Rock musicians–United States–Biography–Juvenile literature. [1. Holly, Buddy, 1936-1959. 2. Musicians. 3. Rock music.] I. Cyrus, Kurt, ill. II. Title.
ML3930.H65 B87 2005
782.42166'092–dc22
2003019270

first
edition

A time or two ago, out West Texas way, where
tumbleweeds rolled down flat, dusty streets and the sunny
sun and the starry stars shined brighter than bright, a
good-hearted family howdied their newest young'un into
this ol' world. They named him Charles Hardin after his
granddaddy Charles and his granddaddy Hardin.

But his mama called him Buddy.

It was the Great Depression. His family might've been money poor, but little Buddy was rich in love. And in music, too.

Ooooo-eeeee, could his kin sing.

At night they'd raise soaring-to-the-heavens hymns plus toe-tappin', boot-stompin' western tunes.

They'd play piano, violin, and accordion, too.

Everyone except his daddy, who'd say, "Someone has to listen."

Music set deep in Buddy's bones. Why, when he was barely knee-high to an armadillo, he play-fiddled and sang at a talent contest. Boy, howdy! Just five years old and he lassoed first prize.

But music wasn't top dog for Buddy during his early schoolin' years. No, siree.

He fancied hittin' homers in the red, red dirt.
Thwack. Smack. Thwack.

Peltin' cans with his slingshot.
Ping. Pang. Ping.

Chasin' Alonzo.
Yap. Yap. Yap.

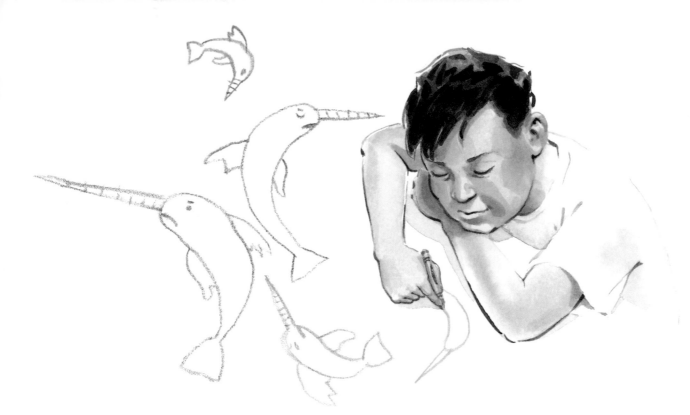

He loved drawin' pictures. Aaah. Oooo. Aaah.

Readin' comics. Kapow. Zow.
And divin' into adventure stories too. Yippee.

He might've been quiet as a jackrabbit, but he was always a-lookin', always a-listenin', always a-tryin'. His mama told him he could do anything he put his mind to.

Buddy might've been the smallest of his kin, but he was always a-reachin' higher.

When it came time for piano, though, Buddy hopped away quicker than a cricket. He was too busy ridin' in a soapbox derby.

Shootin' marbles.

Waitin' on fish.

But come sixth grade . . .

his parents got him a guitar.

Mmm-mm.

He strummed,

he picked,

he twanged....

Buddy stuck to that guitar like white on rice. He played and played and played some more. Mostly he taught himself. His fingers hightailed it down those strings.

Any old time. Any old where. He'd play. And play. Whoo-de-doo. That guitar set Buddy's spirits a-soarin'. Soarin' on the windy wind.

Buddy dreamed dreams bigger than the wide-open West Texas sky, and music makin' was deep in his heart.

Yes, siree.

Any old time. Any old where. He'd play. And play some more.

Country and gospel ran through Buddy's veins. He learned from family and by listening to his favorites: country boys Hank Williams, Bill Monroe, and Bob Wills. After hearing a song, he'd give it his own twist, stretching out a word farther than f-aaa-r, adding hic-hic-cups between sounds. Making it his.

By the time Buddy was a teenager, his heart had begun a-beatin' to a sound called rhythm and blues. **Doe-ing, doe-ing, doe-iiiiiing.** Late at night, beneath a heaven full of stars, he'd listen to the radio play Muddy Waters and Lightnin' Hopkins. Buddy had no doubt about it—those cats electrified the airwaves with their jivin', wailin' ways. Just days past Buddy's seventeenth birthday, he and his pal Jack were asked to sing and play on a weekly local radio show. Now Buddy had radio fans of his own.

It wasn't long before Buddy
heard a newfangled commotion.
Oh-yeah. Oooh-yeaaaaaaah.
Its fast-driving, pounding beat spun off the
turntable and shook up the stage. It was country, gospel,
and blues all fired into one. Hot-diggity! Rock 'n' roll!
Yeehaw! It was cooler than cool. When a young
singer named Elvis Presley performed in Lubbock,
Buddy and his friend Bob opened the show.
That Buddy always made things his own. Even
though no music star wore glasses, Buddy did.
Then he put away his cowboy boots and just
before graduation got himself a Fender
Stratocaster electric guitar.

Faster than greased lightnin', louder than a thunderstorm, more powerful than a Texas twister, and plumb full of gumption, Buddy and his friends wrote and played hip-hoppin' tunes. No foolin'. That music blasted them into out-of-this-world places.

Any old time. Any old where. They'd rock. Buddy took his guitar and let it lead the way.

If it was a sound they hadn't reckoned with before, it was all the better.

Yeeee-dogie. Buddy might've been a tad shy, but put him onstage and he'd light up like Christmas. Creatin' something sparklin' new with his band—that felt star-spangled special. Chasin' notes. Catchin' words. Puttin' them together just so. Hopin' for a cracklin' grand finale. Pa-BOOM. Pa-POW. Aaah-OOO. Oooh-WOW.

Reachin'. Reachin' for the starry stars.

Comin' home after a gig, Buddy would find his mama a-waitin' for their "jam session"—a peanut butter and jelly sandwich.

Buddy's mama thought his music was the greatest thing since do-re-mi.

Not everyone thought rock 'n' roll was as fine as dollar cotton.

"A fad," said some.

"Too wild," said others.

"Mighty loud," said many.

"Too different," said more.

Buddy wondered if his dreams would ever come true. But he kept at it still.

Then the year after graduation, Buddy was signed to make his first record. It was a big break. And the phone kept ringing.

That'll be the day . . .
Buddy had learned music at his mama's knee.
Words of love . . .
Buddy's heart beat strong to the music.
Believe me . . .
Buddy felt music in his bones.
It's a wonderful feeling . . .
Buddy lived his music.
Not fade away . . .
Buddy *was* his music.
Everyday . . .
Peggy Sue . . .
Oh, boy! . . .

Upbeat as a sunrise, Buddy and his band kept a-rollin'.
New York. Austin. San Diego. Alberta. And everywhere in
between. Fans stomped, clapped, and shouted, "More!"

Any old time. Any old where. They called themselves
Buddy Holly and the Crickets: now Jerry, Joe B., Niki, and
Buddy. They'd rock. On and on.

Catchy tunes kept a-comin',
bedazzlin' Buddy with their bright,
bouncy beat.
Freer than the windy wind.
Buddy Holly soared.
And soared.
Oooo-ooo.

Buddy Holly was born on September 7, 1936, in Lubbock, Texas. At birth his full name was Charles Hardin Holley. When an early recording contract misspelled Buddy's last name as "Holly," he dropped the "e".

Growing up, Buddy Holly had many friends he played music with: Bob Montgomery, Larry Welborn, and Jack Neal. In 1953, Jack and Buddy had their own live radio show on KDAV in Lubbock. In 1954, Jack left and was replaced by Bob. Later Larry joined the duo.

On February 13, 1955, "Buddy and Bob," as they were then named, opened for Elvis Presley at the Fair Park Coliseum.

Always making new bands, Buddy Holly also played with Sonny Curtis and Don Guess before he formed the Crickets.

Buddy Holly signed his first recording contract with Decca Records on January 25, 1956. His Nashville recording sessions of that year were not a huge success, and he taped his early hits in a Clovis, New Mexico, studio. Even so, not all of the songs that he recorded were released. Some songs featured Buddy Holly as a background vocalist, and others, like "Believe Me" and "It's a Wonderful Feeling," featured him as an instrumentalist.

When Buddy Holly formed the Crickets in 1957, he and the other band members, Jerry (J. I.) Allison, Joe B. Mauldin, and Niki Sullivan decided they wanted an insect name, consulted an encyclopedia, and chose "Crickets" because "they make a happy sound."

Buddy Holly and the Crickets' first hit, "That'll Be the Day," topped the *Billboard* chart in 1957. That next year alone they had seven Top Forty hit singles.

Over time the group fluctuated between three and four members. They also included Sonny Curtis, Larry Welborn, Tommy Allsup, Carl Bunch, and Waylon Jennings.

Buddy Holly is remembered as a rock 'n' roll pioneer. Corralling together a drummer, bass player, and two guitarists for a rock 'n' roll band was a first. Eventually new groups such as the Beatles and the Rolling Stones followed the lead of Buddy Holly and the Crickets.

With trailblazing arrangements including instruments such as a celesta, strings, and even a cardboard box, Buddy Holly and his band opened up new territory—using overdubbing and double-tracking recording techniques, methods that were novelties at the time.

Buddy Holly died in a plane crash on February 3, 1959, at the age of twenty-two.

Discography of Buddy Holly and the Crickets

TOP U.S. *BILLBOARD* AND *CASHBOX* HIT SINGLES

"That'll Be the Day" (Decca) 1957

"Peggy Sue" (Coral) 1957

"Oh, Boy!" (Brunswick) 1957

"Everyday" (Coral) 1957

"Maybe Baby" (Brunswick) 1958

"Rave On" (Coral) 1958

"Think It Over" (Brunswick) 1958

"Early in the Morning" (Coral) 1958

"Fool's Paradise" (Brunswick) 1958

"Heartbeat" (Coral) 1958

TOP LONG-PLAYING RECORD ALBUM HITS

The Buddy Holly Story (Coral) 1959

Reminiscing (Coral) 1963

Bibliography

Ayers, Samuel J. *Buddy Holly: A Legacy of Music.* Lubbock, TX: Hermosa Creations, 1999.

Goldrosen, John, and John Beecher. *Remembering Buddy: The Definitive Biography of Buddy Holly.* New York: Viking, 1986.

Griggs, Bill. *Buddy Holly Day-by-Day: Book One.* Lubbock, TX: ROCKIN' 50s, 1997.

Lehmer, Larry. *The Day the Music Died: The Last Tour of Buddy Holly, the "Big Bopper," and Ritchie Valens.* New York: Schirmer Books, 1997.

Mann, Alan. *Elvis & Buddy: Linked Lives.* Yorkshire, England: Music Mentor Books, 2002.

Norman, Philip. *Buddy: The Biography.* New York: Macmillan, 1996.

Web Sites

Buddy Holly Center

www.buddyhollycenter.org

The History of Rock 'n' Roll: Buddy Holly and The Crickets

www.history-of-rock.com/buddy_holly.htm

The Official Web Site: Buddy Holly

www.buddyholly.com

Rock and Roll Hall of Fame and Museum

www.rockhall.com